BARITONE B.C.

HOLIDAY FAVORITES

Solos and Band Arrangements
Correlated with Essential Elements® Band Method

Arranged by ROBERT LONGFIELD, JOHNNIE VINSON, MICHAEL SWEENEY and PAUL LAVENDER

T0081644

Welcome to Essential Elements Holiday Favorites! There are two versions of each selection in this versatile book. The SOLO version appears in the beginning of each student book. The FULL BAND arrangement of each song follows. The ONLINE RECORDINGS or PIANO ACCOMPANIMENT BOOK may be used as an accompaniment for solo performance. Use these recordings when playing solos for friends and family.

PLAYBACK+
Speed • Pitch • Balance • Loop

To access audio visit:
www.halleonard.com/mylibrary

Enter Code
1055-8908-9176-9918

ISBN 978-1-5400-2798-6

Hal•Leonard®

Visit Hal Leonard Online at
www.halleonard.com

00870016

Contact Us:
Hal Leonard
7777 West Bluemound Road
Milwaukee, WI 53213
Email: info@halleonard.com

In Europe contact:
Hal Leonard Europe Limited
42 Wigmore Street
Marylebone, London, W1U 2RN
Email: info@halleonardeurope.com

In Australia contact:
Hal Leonard Australia Pty. Ltd.
4 Lentara Court
Cheltenham, Victoria, 3192 Australia
Email: info@halleonard.com.au

AULD LANG SYNE

BARITONE B.C.
Solo

Words by ROBERT BURNS
Traditional Scottish Melody
Arranged by MICHAEL SWEENEY

00870016

FELIZ NAVIDAD

BARITONE B.C.
Solo

Music and Lyrics by
JOSÉ FELICIANO
Arranged by PAUL LAVENDER

00870016

PARADE OF THE WOODEN SOLDIERS

BARITONE B.C.
Solo

English Lyrics by BALLARD MacDONALD
Music by LEON JESSEL
Arranged by PAUL LAVENDER

GOOD KING WENCESLAS

BARITONE B.C.
Solo

Words by JOHN M. NEALE
Music from PIAE CANTIONES
Arranged by ROBERT LONGFIELD

PAT-A-PAN
(Willie, Take Your Little Drum)

BARITONE B.C.
Solo

Words and Music by
BERNARD de la MONNOYE
Arranged by ROBERT LONGFIELD

00870016

SILVER BELLS

BARITONE B.C.
Solo

Words and Music by
JAY LIVINGSTON and **RAY EVANS**
Arranged by PAUL LAVENDER

00870016

DO YOU HEAR WHAT I HEAR

BARITONE B.C.
SOLO

Words and Music by
NOEL REGNEY and GLORIA SHAYNE
Arranged by MICHAEL SWEENEY

00870016

From THE SOUND OF MUSIC
MY FAVORITE THINGS

BARITONE B.C.
Solo

Lyrics by OSCAR HAMMERSTEIN II
Music by RICHARD RODGERS
Arranged by ROBERT LONGFIELD

00870016

From the Motion Picture Irving Berlin's HOLIDAY INN

WHITE CHRISTMAS

BARITONE B.C.
Solo

Words and Music by
IRVING BERLIN
Arranged by JOHNNIE VINSON

CHRISTMAS TIME IS HERE

BARITONE B.C.
Solo

Words by LEE MENDELSON
Music by VINCE GUARALDI
Arranged by JOHNNIE VINSON

From Warner Bros. Pictures' THE POLAR EXPRESS

THE POLAR EXPRESS

BARITONE B.C.
Solo

Words and Music by
GLEN BALLARD and **ALAN SILVESTRI**
Arranged by JOHNNIE VINSON

AULD LANG SYNE

BARITONE B.C.
Band Arrangement

Words by ROBERT BURNS
Traditional Scottish Melody
Arranged by MICHAEL SWEENEY

00870016

FELIZ NAVIDAD

BARITONE B.C.
Band Arrangement

Music and Lyrics by
JOSÉ FELICIANO
Arranged by PAUL LAVENDER

PARADE OF THE WOODEN SOLDIERS

English Lyrics by BALLARD MacDONALD
Music by LEON JESSEL
Arranged by PAUL LAVENDER

BARITONE B.C.
Band Arrangement

00870016

GOOD KING WENCESLAS

BARITONE B.C.
Band Arrangement

Words by JOHN M. NEALE
Music from PIAE CANTIONES
Arranged by ROBERT LONGFIELD

00870016

PAT-A-PAN
(Willie, Take Your Little Drum)

BARITONE B.C.
Band Arrangement

Words and Music by
BERNARD de la MONNOYE
Arranged by ROBERT LONGFIELD

SILVER BELLS

BARITONE B.C.
Band Arrangement

Words and Music by
JAY LIVINGSTON and RAY EVANS
Arranged by PAUL LAVENDER

DO YOU HEAR WHAT I HEAR

BARITONE B.C.
Band Arrangement

Words and Music by
NOEL REGNEY and GLORIA SHAYNE
Arranged by MICHAEL SWEENEY

00870016

From THE SOUND OF MUSIC

MY FAVORITE THINGS

BARITONE B.C.
Band Arrangement

Lyrics by OSCAR HAMMERSTEIN II
Music by RICHARD RODGERS
Arranged by ROBERT LONGFIELD

From the Motion Picture Irving Berlin's HOLIDAY INN

WHITE CHRISTMAS

BARITONE B.C.
Band Arrangement

Words and Music by
IRVING BERLIN
Arranged by JOHNNIE VINSON

1. (Optional repeat)

2. **38** Slower

CHRISTMAS TIME IS HERE

BARITONE B.C.
Band Arrangement

Words by LEE MENDELSON
Music by VINCE GUARALDI
Arranged by JOHNNIE VINSON

THE POLAR EXPRESS

BARITONE B.C.
Band Arrangement

Words and Music by
GLEN BALLARD and ALAN SILVESTRI
Arranged by JOHNNIE VINSON

00870016